SOUND INNOVATIONS

ENSEMBLE DEVELOPMENT

Chorales and Warm-up Exercises for Tone, Technique and Rhythm

YOUNG CONCERT BAND

Peter **BOONSHAFT** | Chris **BERNOTAS**

Thank you for making *Sound Innovations Ensemble Development for Young Concert Band* a part of your large ensemble curriculum. With 167 exercises, including more than 100 chorales by some of today's most renowned young band composers, this book will be a valuable resource in helping you grow in your understanding and abilities as an ensemble musician.

An assortment of exercises, grouped by key, are presented in a variety of young band difficulty levels. Where possible, several exercises in the same category are provided to allow variety while accomplishing the goals of that specific type of exercise. You will notice that many exercises and chorales are clearly marked with dynamics, articulations, style and tempo for you to practice those aspects of performance. Other exercises are intentionally left for you or your teacher to determine how best to use them in reaching your performance goals.

Whether you are progressing through exercises to better your technical facility or challenging your musicianship with beautiful chorales, we are confident you will be excited, motivated and inspired by using *Sound Innovations Ensemble Development for Young Concert Band*.

© 2016 Alfred Music
Sound Innovations® is a registered trademark of Alfred Music
All Rights Reserved including Public Performance

ISBN-10: 1-4706-3393-0
ISBN-13: 978-1-4706-3393-6

Instrument photos courtesy of Yamaha Corporation of America Band & Orchestral Division

Concert B♭ Major (Your C Major)

1 **LONG TONES**

2 **PASSING THE TONIC**

3 **PASSING THE TONIC**

4 **PITCH MATCHING: WOODWIND MOUTHPIECES WITH BAND ACCOMPANIMENT**

5 **SCALE BUILDER**

6 **SCALE BUILDER**

7 EXPANDING INTERVALS: DIATONIC

8 EXPANDING INTERVALS: CHROMATIC

9 INTERVAL BUILDER: DIATONIC INTERVALS

10 INTERVAL BUILDER: PERFECT INTERVALS

11 CHORD BUILDER

12 CHORD BUILDER

13 MOVING CHORD TONES

4

14 DIATONIC HARMONY

15 DIATONIC HARMONY

16 RHYTHMIC SOUNDS

Play the repeated section at least 4 times.

Start 3rd time

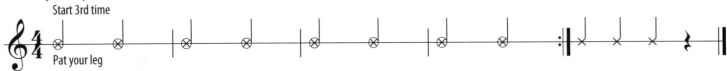

Pat your leg

17 RHYTHMIC SUBDIVISION

18 5-NOTE SCALE

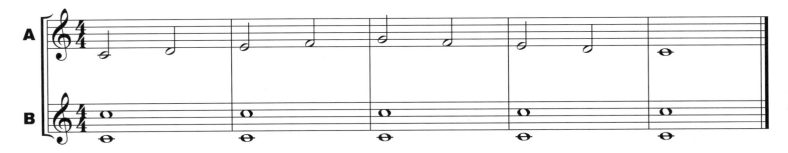

19 CANON: 5-NOTE SCALE

20 CANON: 6-NOTE SCALE

21 CANON: 8-NOTE SCALE

22 **CHORALE: 5-NOTE SCALE**

Chris M. Bernotas (ASCAP)

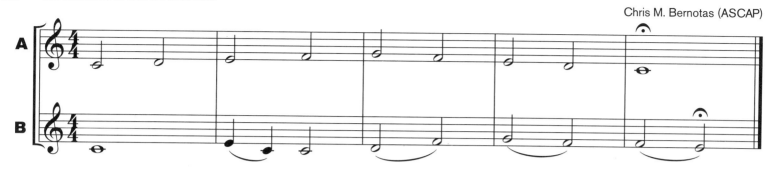

23 **CHORALE: 5-NOTE SCALE**

Chris M. Bernotas (ASCAP)

24 **CHORALE: 6-NOTE SCALE**

Chris M. Bernotas (ASCAP)

25 **CHORALE: 8-NOTE SCALE**

Chris M. Bernotas (ASCAP)

26 **CHORALE: 8-NOTE SCALE**

Chris M. Bernotas (ASCAP)

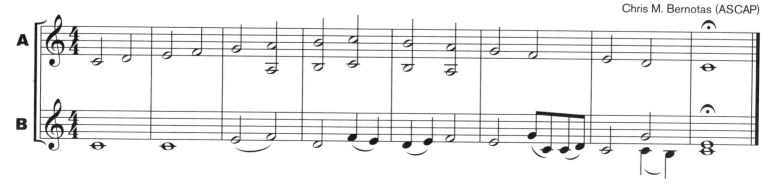

6

27 CHORALE

Robert Sheldon (ASCAP)

28 CHORALE

John O'Reilly (ASCAP)

Moderato

29 CHORALE

Ralph Ford (ASCAP)

30 CHORALE

Michael Story (ASCAP)

Moderately

31 CHORALE

Randall D. Standridge (ASCAP)

32 CHORALE

Roland Barrett (ASCAP)

33 CHORALE

Chris M. Bernotas (ASCAP)

Slowly

34 CHORALE

Rob Grice (ASCAP)

35 CHORALE
Very smoothly
Matt Conaway (ASCAP)

36 CHORALE
Largo
Scott Watson (BMI)

37 CHORALE
Maestoso
Todd Stalter (ASCAP)

38 CHORALE
Robert Sheldon (ASCAP)

39 CHORALE
Moderately
Tyler S. Grant (ASCAP)

40 CHORALE
Randall D. Standridge (ASCAP)

41 CHORALE
Maestoso
Todd Stalter (ASCAP)

42 CHORALE
Moderately slow
Michael Story (ASCAP)

8

43 CHORALE

Ralph Ford (ASCAP)

44 CHORALE

John O'Reilly (ASCAP)

Andante

45 CHORALE

"Finally the first smells of Summer were in the air. 'Time to plant those strange seeds we found,' she thought."

Jodie Blackshaw (ASCAP)

46 CHORALE

Matt Conaway (ASCAP)

Gently flowing

47 CHORALE

Randall D. Standridge (ASCAP)

48 CHORALE

Robert Sheldon (ASCAP)

49 CHORALE

Chris M. Bernotas (ASCAP)

Slowly

50 CHORALE

Roland Barrett (ASCAP)

Concert G Minor (Your A Minor)

51 LONG TONES

52 PASSING THE TONIC

53 EXPANDING INTERVALS: DIATONIC

54 INTERVAL BUILDER: DIATONIC INTERVALS

55 CHORD BUILDER

56 DIATONIC HARMONY

57 CHORALE: 5-NOTE SCALE

Chris M. Bernotas (ASCAP)

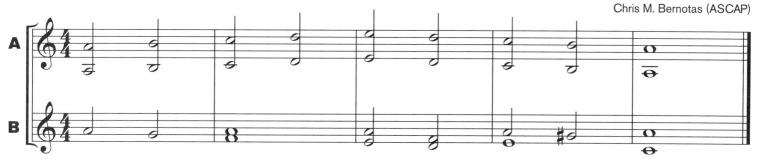

58 CHORALE: 8-NOTE SCALE (NATURAL MINOR)

Chris M. Bernotas (ASCAP)

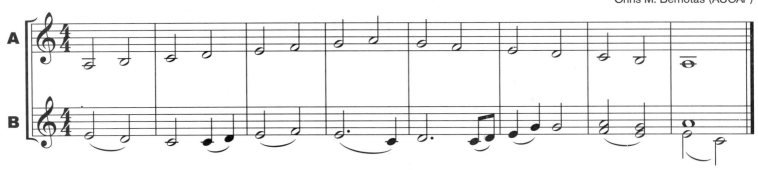

59 CHORALE: 8-NOTE SCALE (HARMONIC MINOR)

Chris M. Bernotas (ASCAP)

60 CHORALE

Tyler S. Grant (ASCAP)

Flowing

61 CHORALE

Rob Grice (ASCAP)

62 CHORALE

Robert Sheldon (ASCAP)

63 CHORALE

Michael Story (ASCAP)

Moderately slow

64 CHORALE

Randall D. Standridge (ASCAP)

Concert E♭ Major (Your F Major)

73 **LONG TONES**

74 **LONG TONES**

75 **PASSING THE TONIC**

76 **PASSING THE TONIC**

77 **SCALE BUILDER**

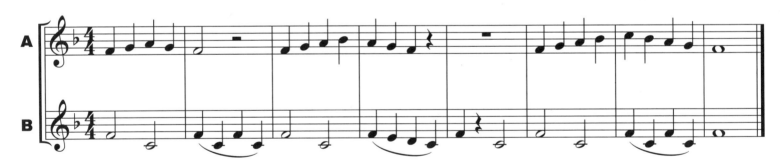

78 **SCALE BUILDER**

79 EXPANDING INTERVALS: DIATONIC

80 EXPANDING INTERVALS: CHROMATIC

81 INTERVAL BUILDER: DIATONIC INTERVALS

82 INTERVAL BUILDER: PERFECT INTERVALS

83 CHORD BUILDER

84 CHORD BUILDER

85 MOVING CHORD TONES

86 DIATONIC HARMONY

87 DIATONIC HARMONY

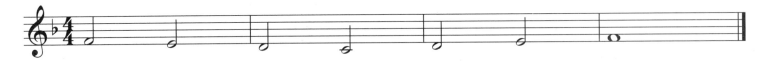

88 RHYTHMIC SUBDIVISION

89 5-NOTE SCALE

90 CANON: 5-NOTE SCALE

91 CANON: 6-NOTE SCALE

92 CANON: 8-NOTE SCALE

93 **CHORALE: 5-NOTE SCALE**

Chris M. Bernotas (ASCAP)

94 **CHORALE: 5-NOTE SCALE**

Chris M. Bernotas (ASCAP)

95 **CHORALE: 6-NOTE SCALE**

Chris M. Bernotas (ASCAP)

96 **CHORALE: 8-NOTE SCALE**

Chris M. Bernotas (ASCAP)

97 **CHORALE: 8-NOTE SCALE**

Chris M. Bernotas (ASCAP)

16

98 CHORALE

Todd Stalter (ASCAP)

99 CHORALE

Michael Story (ASCAP)

100 CHORALE

Rob Grice (ASCAP)

101 CHORALE

Matt Conaway (ASCAP)

102 CHORALE

John O'Reilly (ASCAP)

103 CHORALE

Scott Watson (BMI)

104 CHORALE

Roland Barrett (ASCAP)

105 CHORALE

Ralph Ford (ASCAP)

106 CHORALE

Rob Grice (ASCAP)

107 CHORALE

Tyler S. Grant (ASCAP)

Andante rubato

108 CHORALE

Chris M. Bernotas (ASCAP)

Slowly

109 CHORALE

Robert Sheldon (ASCAP)

110 CHORALE

Todd Stalter (ASCAP)

Maestoso

111 CHORALE

Jodie Blackshaw (ASCAP)

"In the mist there lurked a dark shadowy figure. Could it be?"

poco rit.

112 CHORALE

Matt Conaway (ASCAP)

113 CHORALE

Tyler S. Grant (ASCAP)

Concert C Minor (Your D Minor)

122 LONG TONES

123 PASSING THE TONIC

124 EXPANDING INTERVALS: DIATONIC

125 INTERVAL BUILDER: DIATONIC INTERVALS

126 CHORD BUILDER

127 DIATONIC HARMONY

128 CHORALE: 5-NOTE SCALE

Chris M. Bernotas (ASCAP)

129 **CHORALE: 8-NOTE SCALE (NATURAL MINOR)**

Chris M. Bernotas (ASCAP)

130 **CHORALE: 8-NOTE SCALE (HARMONIC MINOR)**

Chris M. Bernotas (ASCAP)

131 **CHORALE**

Tyler S. Grant (ASCAP)

Slowly

132 **CHORALE**

Rob Grice (ASCAP)

133 **CHORALE**

Ralph Ford (ASCAP)

134 **CHORALE**

Robert Sheldon (ASCAP)

135 **CHORALE**

Michael Story (ASCAP)

Moderately slow

136 CHORALE

Scott Watson (BMI)

137 CHORALE

Matt Conaway (ASCAP)

138 CHORALE

Rob Grice (ASCAP)

139 CHORALE

Chris M. Bernotas (ASCAP)

Largo

140 CHORALE

Randall D. Standridge (ASCAP)

141 CHORALE

"Through the haze they glared at each other. He'd been waiting a long time for this."

Jodie Blackshaw (ASCAP)

142 CHORALE

Roland Barrett (ASCAP)

143 CHORALE

John O'Reilly (ASCAP)

Adagio

22

Concert F Major (Your G Major)

144 PASSING THE TONIC

145 EXPANDING INTERVALS: CHROMATIC

146 CHORD BUILDER

147 DIATONIC HARMONY

148 CHORALE: 6-NOTE SCALE

Chris M. Bernotas (ASCAP)

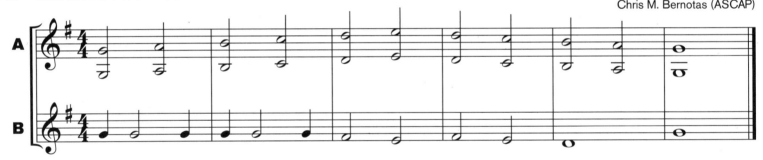

149 CHORALE

Rob Grice (ASCAP)

150 CHORALE

Ralph Ford (ASCAP)

151 CHORALE

Scott Watson (BMI)

152 CHORALE

Randall D. Standridge (ASCAP)

153 CHORALE

John O'Reilly (ASCAP)

Andante

154 CHORALE

Roland Barrett (ASCAP)

155 CHORALE

Adapted from Psalm 150, Claude Goudimel
Arranged by Todd Stalter (ASCAP)

Maestoso

Concert D Minor (Your E Minor)

156 PASSING THE TONIC

157 CHORD BUILDER

158 DIATONIC HARMONY

159 CHORALE: 8-NOTE SCALE (HARMONIC MINOR)

Chris M. Bernotas (ASCAP)

24

160 CHORALE

Roland Barrett (ASCAP)

161 CHORALE

Robert Sheldon (ASCAP)

162 CHORALE

Todd Stalter (ASCAP)

Maestoso

1

2

163 CHORALE

Scott Watson (BMI)

Adagio

1

2

rit.

rit.

164 CHORALE

Michael Story (ASCAP)

Moderately slow

165 CHORALE

Ralph Ford (ASCAP)

166 CHORALE

Tyler S. Grant (ASCAP)

167 CHORALE

Jodie Blackshaw (ASCAP)

"In the darkness all she could hear was the sound of her beating heart. What had she done?"